D1220727

The Compleat Melancholick

THE
COMPLEAT MELANCHOLICK

Being

A Sequence of

Found, Composite, and Composed

POEMS,

based largely upon

Robert Burton's

The Anatomy of Melancholy,

by

LEWIS TURCO

Published by The Bieler Press
Minneapolis

This project has been supported through a grant from
the National Endowment for the Arts in Washington, D.C.,
a federal agency.

LIBRARY OF CONGRESS CATALOGING IN PUBLICATION DATA

Turco, Lewis.
    The compleat melancholick.

        I. Melancholy—Poetry.   I. Burton, Robert, 1577-1640.
The anatomy of melancholy.   II. Title.
PS3570.U626C58   1985   811'.54   82-22742
ISBN 0-931460-12-3 (limited edition)
ISBN 0-931460-15-8 (paperback)

These poems, in various versions variously titled, originally appeared in the following periodicals, to the editors and publishers of which the author owes acknowledgement and thanks: *The Carleton Miscellany* for "The Melancholick Art" (under the title "Thoughts on Writing While Trying to Write"); *Commonweal* and *Fragments* for "The Garden of Melancholy" ("The Garden"); *Concerning Poetry* for "The Mistress of Melancholy"; *De Paul Literary Magazine* for "A Squis'd Cat" ("Louis Wain's Cats"); *Iowa Review* for "The Desert of Melancholy"; *Johns Hopkins Magazine* and *Striver's Row* for "Winter in Muscovy"; *La Fusta* for "Failed Fathers"; *La Huerta* for "The God of Melancholy" ("The Laughing God"); *Loon* for "The Symptons of Melancholy"; *Modern Poetry Studies* for "Farewell to Melancholy"; *M. S. S.* for "A Fin for the Melcholick's Thoughts" ("A Fin for the Professor's Thoughts"); *New York Quarterly* for "The Menu of Melancholy"; *New Collage* for "Melancholy Love"; *Northwest Review* for "The Mandarin of Melancholy" ("The Mandarin of Silence"); *Poetry* for "Some Food for Melancholy" ("Some Food for Thought"); *Poetry Northwest* for "The Author of Melancholy," "Melancholy's Herbal," "The Moon of Melancholy," and "That Particular Air"; *Sam Houston Literary Review* for "Stone and Shadow"; *Studies In Contemporary Satire* for "Emeralda" and "I Pray to a Genital God"; *Three Rivers Poetry Journal* for "Blood Deeper Than Night"; *Voices* for "A Medicine for Melancholy" ("To Smoke a Pipe"), and *Wind* for "Taurus Sires Aquarius" and "The Compleat Melancholick."

The author wishes to acknowledge the Research Foundation of State University of New York for fellowship aids granted in support of the writing of this book, the Yaddo Corporation for a residency during which several of these pieces were written, and the State University of New York College at Oswego for a sabbatical leave in 1979, during which this collection was readied for publication.

Contents

THE COMPLEAT MELANCHOLICK

Melancholy. From the Augsburg Calendar (about 1480)

IN ORDER TO AVOID MELANCHOLY, Robert Burton says
in his *The Anatomy of Melancholy* (1628), one *May apply
his mind, I say, to Heraldry, Antiquity, invent Impresses,
Emblems; make Epithalamiums, Epitaphs, Elegies, Epi-
grams, Palindromes, Anagrams, Chronograms, Acrosticks
upon his friends' names; or write a comment on Martianus
Capella, Tertullian's Cloak, the Nubian Geography, or up-
on Ælia Laelia Crispis, as many idle fellows have assayed;
and rather than do nothing, vary a verse a thousand ways
with Putean, so torturing his wits, or as Rainnarius of Lune-
berg, 2,150 times in his Proteus Poeticus, or Scaliger,
Chrysolithus, Cleppisius, and others, have in like sort done.*

THE COMPLEAT MELANCHOLICK

—out of Burton

"Of seasons of the year,
the Autumn is most melancholy."
Then lovers lie within their sheets,
thoughts winding among their separations,
dreaming of darknesses chill enough
"to refrigerate the heart—

"windy melancholy,"
cholick of leaves and limbs, of owlcry
and blue hound moaning at the sky.
"Some persons think that every star's a world,
and call this earth of ours an obscure
star, presided over by the least of

"gods." The lovers dream of
"phrenzy, ecstasy, revelations,
visions, enthusiasms," these
demons of the blood. "The Talmudists say
that Adam had a wife called Lilis,
before he married Eve, &

"of her he begat no
Thing but Dyvils. These unclean spirits
settled in our bodies, and now
mixed with our melancholy humours, do
triumph as it were, and sport themselves
as in another heaven.

"Cauls, kells, tunicles, creeks"
are their changelings for our desires. "By
their charms they can draw down the moon
from the heavens." The lovers?—they lie to
wish. "This humour of Melancholy
is called the Devil's Bath." You

least of Gods, this is
a petty Hell: These solitary
pallets beneath the falling moon.
I conjure you, with little charm, "Bring their
sweethearts to them by night, upon a
goat's back flying in the air."

The Menu of Melancholy

—out of Burton

These do generally ingender gross humours
      and windy bile, fill "all those inward parts
    with obstructions: Beef, goat's flesh (a filthy beast,
and rammish); hart & red deer hath an evil name,
      it yields gross nutriment, next unto horse";

all venison is melancholy, and begets
      bad blood; hare breeds incubus; conies are
    of the like nature; pork "may breed a quartan
ague." All fish are discommended, for they breed
      "viscosities, slimy nutriment, lit-

"tle and humourous nutriment; eel, tench, lamprey,
      crawfish; all fish, that standing pools and lakes
    frequent, yield bad juice and nourishment, dried, soused,
indurate fish, as ling, fumadoes, red herrings,
      sprats, stockfish, haberdine, poor-John; all shell

"fish, conger, sturgeon, turbot, mackerel, skate. Amongst
      fowl, peacocks and pigeons, all fenny fowl
    are forbidden, as ducks, geese, swans, herns, cranes, coots,
didappers, waterhens, with all those teals, curs, shel-
      drakes, and peckled fowls." Among herbs: "Gourds, cow-

"cumbers, coleworts, melons, cabbage; all raw herbs and
      sallets breed melancholy blood; roots &
    sole food are windy and bad, or troublesome

to the head; as onions, garlick, scallions, turnips,
    carrots, radishes, parsnips. All manner

"of fruits" are forbidden, "as pears, apples, cherries,
        plums, strawberries, nuts, medlers, serves, sweetings,
    pearmains, pippins, grapes & figs. All pulse are naught:
beans, pease, fitches &c."—they fill the brain with gross
        "fumes, breed black thick blood," cause troublous dreams. Of

"spices: Pepper, ginger, cinnamon, cloves, mace, dates,
        honey and sugar; all aromatics,
    all sharp & sour things, luscious & oversweet,
or fat, as oil, vinegar, verjuice, mustard, salt;
        bread of baser grain, as pease, beans, oats, rye,

"or overhard baked, crusty & black, oats and corn.
        All black wines; overhot, compound, strong drinks,
    as Muscadine, Malmsey, Alicant, Rumney,
Brown Bastard, Metheglin, Cyder & Perry. Beer
        overnew or over stale, over strong

"or not sod, that smells of the cask, sharp or sour—
        it frets and galls because of the hop." And
    compound dishes beyond these simples: "Puddings
stuffed with blood, baked meats, soused, indurate meats fried &
        broiled; condite; milk, and all that comes of milk,

"—cheese, curds; all cakes, simnels, buns, cracknels, made with spice,
        butter, &c.; fritters, pancakes,

pies, sausages, & those several sauces, sharp
or oversweet." And waters last: "Standing waters,
        thick & ill-colored, such as come forth of

"pools and moats, where hemp hath been steeped or fishes live,
        are most unwholesome, putrefied, full of
    mites, creepers, slimy, muddy, unclean, corrupt,
impure." All are windy, full of melancholy.
        Shun them by dawn and dusk, by dark and light.

THE AUTHOR OF MELANCHOLY

*"...idleness, (the badge of gentry),..the bane of body
and mind, the Nurse of Naughtiness, Stepmother of Disci-
pline, the chief Author of all Mischief, one of the
Seven Deadly Sins...the Devil's cushion, as Gualter calls
it, his pillow and chief reposal."*—Burton.

I have put on my badge, and I repose me
upon this pillow beside my gross Familiar.
     My Nurse attends me— coffee, mead, or bile?
      I am in good Humour.

  The room grows close with folk: Stepmother waddles
among the lamps, tobacco thick as bats. Gualter
     and Burton hover above the Author,
      bid him take but little

  notice of the Nurse—or, better—none at all.
"Aquarius saddens the now turned year: The time
     requires, and the Autumn breeds it." One's arse
      begins to itch, digits

  cramp; Stepmother leaves the room. Burton suggests,
"They wear their brains in their bellies, and their guts in
     their heads," these revelers in idleness:
      "Who can drink most, and fox

  "his fellow soonest?" I belch and nudge my pen.
The Seven Sins dance slyly through my spheres. My tongue

is thick, my ink stumbles among these leaves,
    "somniferous potions,

   "knots, amulets, words, philters. They that stutter
and are bald will be soonest melancholy, by
    reason of the dryness of their brains." I
      can no longer see, nor

   may I breathe, so thick has grown the air with these
bleak phantasms of the skull. "Circumforanean
    Rogues and Gipsies ride in the air upon
      a coulstaff out of a

   "chimney-top." Enow! I will be idle hence,
though "the mind can never rest, but still meditates
    on one thing or other; except it be
      occupied about some

   "honest business"—one cannot be a common
Scrivener of Verse. "My mind of his own accord
    it rusheth into Melancholy." The
      Devil take his repose.

BLOOD DEEPER THAN NIGHT

...he is born naked, and falls a whining
at the very first, he is swaddled and bound
up like a prisoner, cannot help himself, and
so he continues to his life's end.—Pliny,
as quoted by Burton.

Where have these strangers come from,
     those who cannot sleep?
  This is the bone of one,
and the flesh of another.
  I hold them in my hand
like ivory and velvet.

They are clothed in blood deeper
     than night in the glass.
  They walk about, utter
what I cannot hear. They sink
  and rise. Their substance is
runic—parchment turned to smoke.

They chant in the vein; they tell
     lyrics out of plasm.
  The temple is groined where
they read without light. Under
  the palm they are silent
among their dark alphabets.

When will these strangers walk down
     into my waking?

This is the word of one,
the silence of another.
I hold them in my palm
like parchment and ivory.

THE MOON OF MELANCHOLY

...a silly country fellow...killed his ass for
drinking up the moon, that he might restore
the moon to the world.—Burton.

It was late when they came in
through the gate. He dismounted
beside the water trough, and the donkey
dropped its nose into the moon to drink.

He stood fatigued underneath
the wind scudding high cloud. No
light beyond reflection lit the windows
of the house. The barn soughed. The long grass

of the fields grew longer in
shadow laid over shadow.
The journey had taken forever. For
as long as it takes to remember,

he forgot where he had been,
and then recalled again. He
closed his eyes, listened to the beast drinking,
and was afraid, suspended

in that quiet of the mind.
When he looked again, when wind
had become too hollow against silence,
he found his eyes were opened,

but still he could not see. His
animal had drunk the moon
out of the water. He tried to discern
   clouds, moon, sky, stars, the edge of the wind,

but found there a well into
which he felt himself to be
sinking. It was a vortex no world
   could withstand. In the morning he wept

over the animal that
had carried him home; he wept
in the sun that had risen with him. He
   remembered the image of

bone, restored as the blade sank
homing: The moon floating in
the trough of water and blood, and the wind
   not quite too hollow to bear.

The Symptoms of Melancholy

—out of Burton

"Some signs are secret, some manifest, some
       in the body, some in the mind;
and diversely vary, according to the
       inward or outward causes: Some laugh,
         some weep, some sleep, some dance, some

"sing, some howl, some drink, they are lean, withered,
       hollow-eyed, look old, wrinkled, harsh,
much troubled with wind, and a griping in their
       bellies, or belly-ache, belch often,
         dry bellies; hard, dejected

"looks, flaggy beards, singing of the ears, ver-
       tigo, lightheaded, little or
no sleep, & that interrupt, terrible and
       fearful dreams—continual sharp &
         stinking belchings, as if their

"meat in their stomack were putrefied, or
       that they had eaten fish; absurd
& interrupt dreams, phantasmal visions
       about their eyes, vertiginous, cold
         sweat, apt to tremble, & prone

"to venery; palpitation of the
       heart, a leaping in many parts
of the body, a kind of itching; fixed eyes

and much twinkling of their eyes—they are
very red-faced; they stutter

"most part; headache, a binding heaviness;
much leaping of wind about the
skin, as well as stutting, or tripping in speech;
hollow eyes, gross veins, & broad lips. To
some too, if they be far gone,

"mimical gestures are too familiar,
laughing, grinning, fleering, murmuring,
talking to themselves, with strange faces,
inarticulate voices, excla-
mations, &c. And

"though commonly lean, hirsute, uncheerful
in countenance, withered, and not
so pleasant to behold—dull, heavy, restless,
yet their memories are most part good, they
have happy wits, excellent

"apprehensions. They cannot sleep, they have
mighty and awful watchings; they
do not eat much, yet they are lean, ill liking,
troubled with costiveness, crudities,
oppilations, spitting. Their

"pulse is rare & slow, except it be of
the 'carotides,' which is very

strong. Their urine is most part low colored &
        pale, not much in quantity, and their
                melancholy excrements,

    "in some very much, in others little,
                as the spleen plays his part, and thence
proceeds wind, palpitation of the heart, short
            breath, plenty of humidity in
                the stomack, heaviness of

    "heart, & heartache, & intolerable
                stupidity and dulness of
spirits; their excrements or stool hard, black to
            some, & little. If the liver, heart,
                spleen, brain, be misaffected,

    "as usually they are, diseases
                accompany, as Incubus,
Apoplexy, Epilepsy, Vertigo,
            those frequent wakings and terrible
                dreams, intempestive laughing,

    "weeping, sighing, sobbing, bashfulness, blushing,
                trembling, sweating, swooning. All their
senses are troubled, they think they see, hear, smell
            and touch that which they do not," as who
                does not, come dream or waking?

EMERALDA

To any man who finds it equally easy to chop up a
live dog and a live lettuce I would recommend
suicide at his earliest convenience.—Konrad Lorenz.

    It was difficult. I was starved,
    of course, but still I found it hard,
    for I had raised her from a seed.
  For moral reasons, I am a carnivore,
and in palmier days, before the game had gone,

    I shared my ample store with her.
    Before her germination was
    assured, I fed her one small fly.
  Her roots ate gratefully into the carcass,
and she began to sprout. Later, she had a frog

    I carved for her. Such gratitude!
    Her tender leaves began to come
    to a head: I formed the humus
  about her base and butchered her a guinea
pig, a cat, and then a dog—this latter at

    some risk, for it fought back. But at last
    I chopped it up and fed it to
    my pet, my greeny pet, my great
  green love, my Emeralda, larger than life.
At last she grew so grand, importunate, nothing

would do except a chimpanzee.
I stalked one for hours, and it was
quite clever. It defecated
on me from the treetops. But I was cagey
too, and I cornered it at last. It did not fight,

but offered me its throat. It smiled.
I could not understand that smile,
yet I made it another one,
farther down, upon its throat. Emeralda
flourished, as did the bond between us. Then the game

began to grow scarce and scarcer.
The chimpanzees went first—the trees
were lorn at branch and root: dogs
raised their legs no longer. The cats prowled to search
for the dogs, the guinea pigs for the cats. The frogs

stopped grumping in the swamp. The flies
missed the sound—they went hunting for
the sticky tongues, and dearth came down
to settle on my plot. It was sorrowful—
but I was starving. I've managed to choke her down,

my Emeralda, may the Gods forgive me.

MELANCHOLY'S HERBAL

What a pother have authors made with Roses! What a racket
they have kept! I shall add, red Roses are under Jupiter,
damask under Venus, white under the Moon, and Provence
under the King of France.—Culpepper.

There are others: Black Hellebore, being an herb of Saturn,
   (it is no marvel) is a sullen plant. If taken raw,
   it is safer to purify it "by the art of the
alchymist." It is specified against all Melancholies,
     quartan agues and madness. "The root consisteth
   of numberless black strings all united into one head."

Balm is an herb of Jupiter, under Cancer. Used as "an
   electuary with honey," it drives out "troublesome
   cares," thoughts blooming darkly out of Melancholy or black
choler. It "causeth the mind and heart to be merry," expels
     "those melancholy vapors from the spirits and
   blood which are in the heart and arteries," deep-rooted.

Hops are martial, under the dominion of Mars, that hot-blooded
   planet. They may be "profitably given in long and
   hot agues that rise in fever and blood." Despite its name,
Sow-Fennel (Mercury under Virgo) is indicated
     in cases of "lethargy, frenzy, giddiness
   of the head," its juice mixed with vinegar or rosewater.

Borage and Bugloss are Jupiter's, under Leo. "The leaves,
   flower, and seed," given as cordials, "expel pensiveness
   and Melancholy" if used green. How they strengthen Nature!

Endive is a "fine, cooling, cleansing, jovial plant." It is
        recommended for "faintings, swoonings, and passions
    of the heart." It is conducive to the best of Humours.

But those roses!—what a pother and racket! What elixirs
    and compounds: "Sugar of Roses, Syrup of dry Roses,
    and honey of Roses!" Rose vapor—rosewater cast on
a hot fireshovel and inhaled. Rose hips, rosepetals plucked
        or crushed, fit for all Melancholies: Provence spread
    like damask under Venus, tapestries beneath the Moon!

THE DESERT OF MELANCHOLY

They have myriads in their mouths. —Burton.

It is not far from here to
nowhere. Merely across the furniture.
    We are experiencing
    technical difficulties; please

do not adjust. If there were
ink in this pen, it would be different.
    However, it is not. This,
    then, is a poem written among

furniture, on paper like
a glass screen, pen like a stainless steel steak
    knife. It is a poem made of
    mirrors. In it you will see, if

you look technically, small
creatures dancing on the head of a pin—
    any number of them: I
    have myriads in my mouth. They

do not know that they are there—
no more than we know they are watching us.
    Well, quite a charming place, this,
    wherever: Chairs, tables, the smell

of meat in the air. No one
will wonder at this devastation of

syllables. Who is to be
awed? It is my devastation,

and I am past wonderment.
It is at this point precisely that the
cactus must resume blossom.
If it does not, words will have no

point. Expect nothing. You will
be disappointed in other things. The
desert does not flower.
It is the flower that flowers.

THAT PARTICULAR AIR

How come they to dig up fish bones,
shells, beams, iron-works, many
fathoms under ground, & anchors in
mountains far remote from all seas?
                    —Burton

The hook has let go,
and the conestoga
has rolled down the cliff, along
with the television set. All
the women sorrow,
for their struggle has

been for nothing, which
they have achieved. The men
do not give up. They have yet
to understand that the wagon
train will not get through.
Of course, the wagon

train will not follow
the Tube, it will follow
the script; the prairie schooners
will reach California. There,
the women will gaze
at the Pacific

Ocean; glance, with that
particular air, at

each other, at their men; they
will lie down to have the children
who sit on the shore:
"You owe to yourself
your own destruction."

WINTER IN MUSCOVY

In muscovy…they live in stoves and hot-houses all
winter long.—Burton.

   Open any grate, any glass gate
     on a street of cast iron or glass,
and someone will say, "Hello," out from between
flames or fronds, white teeth smiling in a soot face:
a flowerchild, an elder or alderman,
     a young lady in pince-nez

   with a pot-belly, tendrils in her
     hair—"Hello, come in, enjoy, enjoy
'May-games, Wakes, and Whitsun-Ales!'" All winter long
in their stoves they make feast with "rare devices
to corrivate waters, musick instruments,
     & trisyllable Echoes,

  "again, again, & again repea-
     ted [ted, ted] with myriads of such."
But if ye be melancholick, enter not,
nor lay thine eyes longing on these revelers—
"Let them freely feast, sing and dance, have their Puppet-
     plays, Hobby-horses, Tabers,

  "Crowds, Bag-pipes, play at Ball, and Barley-
     breaks—an Index of Ignorance—let
them go as they are in the Catalogue of
Ignoramus, snorting on a bulk," although

"nothing can be more excellent and pleasant,
        so abstruse and recondite,

   "so bewitching, so miraculous,
    so ravishing, so easy withal
& full of delight" as these baubles of stove-
dwellers, inhabitants of glass houses,
these multifarious "Martian amulets,
        Weapon Salve, Universal

   "Balsams, strange extracts, Elixirs of
    Life," 'cause that's not where It's at; let one
take heed he do not overstretch his wits and
        make a skeleton of himself.

STONE AND SHADOW

...many cannot sleep for Witches and Fascinations,
which are too familiar in some places....—Burton.

It is as still as falling
    in this house of weathers.
Nothing but lamplight and the shadow of my hand
    lie along the page. The clock
        owns everything.

I have been dreaming of the
    woman. She has faces
to burn. The day's fire is black upon the flagging.
    I listen for wind within
        the flue; there is

only the dark sound of coals
    rising to enter night
smoking over the rooftree. Still, the woman is here
    under towels—or standing
        in a wardrobe

among sleeves and lapels.
    I see her eyes clearly
between the strokes of an hour. She is of a size
    and a certain shape. She has
        loved me in time.

Logs lie at the hearth between
    four dark chimes. I would know

her, for it is said "She sees within the stone beneath
the shadow." She is shadow.
And I am stone.

FAILED FATHERS

"On a theme by, and with apologies to, Greg Pape."

Where do all the failed fathers
go? To Albuquerque? Cleveland?
After the slow slide down the drain,
where do they go? After the last
lay-off, the class reunion where they're shown

kissing the matronly Queen
of the Prom, where do they go. Where
do they go, these old young men, these
paunchy guys with the eyes that squint
into the lens at the family picnic,

the fishing expedition
near the falls, the baseball game where
they played second? After the fights,
the money fights, the brief affair,
after the spree and the morning after,

where do the failed fathers go?
Is there a bar where they gather,
is there a bus they all take,
is there a line at the Bureau
where they talk over their sons and daughters,

their Old Ladies turning cold,
the milkmen they caught spending time
drinking coffee in their kitchens?

41

Is there a motel in Cleveland
full of fathers playing poker,

   smoking cigarettes, squinting
at their hands, drinking beer? Is there,
down in Albuquerque, some street
full of walk-up rooms full of dreams
of mowing lawns, of paneling basements,

   propping children on their bikes,
walking down the aisles of markets
pushing shopping carts? Of course, we
know what happens to our mothers,
but where oh where do the failed fathers go?

THE MANDARIN OF MELANCHOLY

Their Lau-sie, Mandarins, Literates, Licentiates, and
such as have raised themselves by their worth, are
their noblemen only,...—Burton.

He is the mandarin of silence:
The wind, drawing through trees, breathes easily,
though this is no light burden. Here, where mountains
curl into forests; here, now,
the wind rests, and mists twist
among the boulders.

Half a bird sings in half a tree. A
half stroke of rain runs down the mist, the cliff
into what remains of any universe
but this. Watching, there is no
sight; listening, there is
no sound beyond this.

43

A FIN FOR THE MELANCHOLICK'S THOUGHTS

We are all prisoners. What is our life but a prison?
We are all imprisoned in an island.—Burton.

                Denuded by the
                desert sea that swells
                and bowls these freshman
combers over inkwells, this winter beach
is clear now for a fortnight. The students
have washed home for the holidays. They swim
                within grottos and
                nets of motherly
                arms. Here and there, a

shell of an office lies stranded upon
the sand, inhabited by a hermit
crab or glued to silence by an eyeless
                jellyfish. Each of
                us—sea urchin or
                flounder—conjures dreams
of capes and codfish in the southern East;
boats and beaches we may never see, where
the sand is unlettered. Where dunes are not

                cumbered with runes of
                an Anglo-Saxon
                origin. We smell
coastal forests whose heaps of leaf need no
correction. There, night spells daylight, and owls
wisely allow cotton mouths and copper

                              heads right of access
                              to marshland inlet,
                              swamp, and bog. Decay,

like a tidal stream, goes slowly there. There
is always new growth. Death wants no doctor
or master where life cures or kills and will
                              not cheat. There's a half-
                              moon-ebb till the fish
                              reschool. Let all old
seahorses squat back on scaling tails, mud
puppies scan aquarium shelves for leaks—
there's sand between our ears. And snakes, and owls.

THE GARDEN OF MELANCHOLY

*What extraordinary virtues are ascribed unto
plants!*—Burton.

In the garden of odd seed, no
    weeds grow—or, if they do grow
      wild, row on row among
the blossoms of good plant and herb
    furrowed and furbelowed,

the beetles snub them. They crawl black,
    mandibles sawing among
      leaves, leaving speckled spoor
where they go. I care for them all—
    weed and beetle, poor old

plant, my trowel and hoe alive
    in the soil, sun drumming
      upon stone, rain in the
patch, wind quickening the nettle,
    lichen greying green moss,

everything springing, springing—"Priest
    pintle and rocket enliven
      the member; the chaste-tree
and waterlily quench the sperm;
    some herbs provoke lust;

"others, as chaste-lamb, extinguish
    seed; poppy causeth sleep, cabbage

46

resisteth drunkenness.
For the head, Aniseeds, Foalfoot,
Betony, Calamint,

"Eye-bright, Lavender, Bays, Roses,
Rue, Sage, Marjoram, Peony;
for the lungs, Calamint,
Liquorice, Hyssop, Horehound,
Water Germander; for

"the heart, Borage, Bugloss, Saffron,
Balm, Basil, Rosemary,
Violet, Roses; for
the stomack, Wormwood, Mints, Betony,
Balm, Centaury, Sorel,

"Purslain; For the liver, Darthspine,
Germander, Agrimony,
Fennel, Endive, Succory,
Liverwort, Barberries; for the
spleen, Maidenhair, Finger-

"fern, Dodder of Thyme, Hop, the rind
of Ash, Betony; for the
kidnies, Grumel, Parsley,
Saxifrage, Plantain, Mallow; for the
womb, Mugwort, Pennyroyal,

"Fetherfew, Savine; for the joints,
  Camomile, S. John's Wort, Rue,
    Organ, Centaury-the-
Less, Cowslips," each seedling and shoot
    finding roothold among

  the darkling world's dark bones.

The Melancholick Art

...no science, no school, no art, no degree; but,
like a trade, every man in private is instructed
of his master.—Burton.

I. *The Conceit of Melancholy.*

If your pen is a colt, freshly watered
at the inkwell, and your pad of foolscap
lies before you like an undrawn map of open country;
if you've fed your colt good provender:
Hay, oats, barley: A barnful of winter stores;

if, I say, you've fed him well on what was
raked and winnowed in the fall, likely you
will write some verses such as these. Outdoors, the pure meadows
reach for the mountains. The colt can smell
springtime, but you have him tethered just inside the

barn. Will the yearling ride? No. Will he pull
staidly at the phaeton? Not with grass
untasted in his world—not unbroken. Let the damn fool
go! Let him whicker at clouds, let him
moon and meander, then. He will be shod at last.

II. *The Master of Melancholy.*

It's like being haunted.
Something's in the air. I know it is.
I can almost feel it nip my nose,

nibble my ear. If I reach out...,
look! Tobacco smoke.

Move a bit. There's a tree
on the lawn. I might write about that,
or the oriole nest hanging like
Aphrodite's teat from one bough.
That's not it, though. The

lamp: Turn it off. Think hard
about shadows, shapes; the movement of
swamp ferns; how dinosaurs lie in mud
but walk still. Nothing. Ideas
rush for the nearest

exit, but where's the flame?
There's a red engine clanging up the
next block. The hell with this. Perhaps I'll
never write again. I'll go to
bed. That always works.

A Medicine For Melancholy

Tobacco divine, rare, superexcellent Tobacco,
which goes far beyond all their panaceas, potable
gold, and philosopher's stones, a sovereign remedy
to all diseases.—Burton.

It ought to be a large old knot hole,
first of all, surrounded by most of the tree.
        Black inside, as though Hell had poked
        a smokestack out between your teeth.

Now, heave a wheeze downstem hard until
you've blown a beachful of igneous grains out
        into the bowl's bayou. Knock them
        onto your palm. Whistle them off

like a ruinous wind. The carpet
will thrive, grow lush as Virginia. Sit back.
        Knuckle off the roof of your root
        cellar where your tobacco, as

loamy as moss, masses and awaits
a spark's attack. Thumb up a balesworth; trammel
        it down deep into the devil's
        eye. Snatch up an eruption now

and spang! Puff a belly full of fumes.
Whoof! Off go angels and satyrs; clouds of them—
        furry thighs and messes of wings
        bearing you off like an orgy.

SOME FOOD FOR MELANCHOLY

*Make a melancholy man fat, as Rhasis saith, and
thou hast finished the cure.*—Burton.

Morning. The sun is a fried egg in a pastel
    spider.* Were it not for the fact that the world,
        today, is a summer meal, one might not
    eat for a month. Seaweed: A garnishment for
    the salad beach. Tongue of an ocean running
        gluttonously through teeth seemingly

reefs, ruining while renewing what it would chew.
    And Time, damn him, Time: The sadistic chef. He
        whose pendulum spatula flips our egg
    over easy, never nicking the yolk, but
    never truly serving it, either. You'd think
        it would burn. It does. Ogle it once:

It will turn the whites of your eyes to quicksilver.
    Let us not eat for a month. That old cook with
        a grimace of ice will not make gourmands
    of gourmets. We can roast him first on the spit
    of our minds. Imagination may make him
        howl with heat in his own oven, just
as Hansel and Gretel cindered the witch in her
    cookie house. We will savor, not salivate.
        But the hostel-mistress sea works her lewd

---

* In New England a *spider* is a cast-iron skillet.

jowls with too much good humour, professional
of her lies. She and the chef run a public
house. They know too well the public taste.

I PRAY TO A GENITAL GOD

Such medicines are to be exploded that consist
of words, characters, spells, and charms, which
can do no good at all, but out of a strong conceit.
                    —Burton.

When I pointed out the pun
   in her poem, she told me to be still.
   It was no pun—in the panorama
of all her work there wasn't a single pun.
        She hated puns.

   She could no longer work, for
      thinking of the pun. "Disruptive," she said,
   "you're being quite disruptive." Rather than
rapture, she found but rupture now, a pun
        upon her page:

   "Cruel and inhuman pun–
      ishment," she said, "to see where less was meant,"
      but so much more than what I'd seen. She could
not write, not even punctuate. I must be
        more genital,

   compassionate, even blind
      to the printed word, for what she *meant* was
   holy—"My god!" she cried, "can't you at least
be a gentleman? The god I meant was Pan!"
        I bowed my head.

54

"I'm sorry," I said, "I saw
you paging what was not there. I've caused you
pain. I did not mean to pan the poem
you thought you wrote, nor even the one I saw.
        I shall be more

    "genteel in future, and if
I see a pomegranate where you meant
only a poem, granite I'll not see
on Shakespeare's tomb, the punography between
        his poignant lines.

    "I shall note the inscription only,
done by the chiseler's hand when he was dead.
To hell with language. I shall bear my soul
tiptoe among the tombs, hope to fall prey to
        a genital god."

TAURUS SIRES AQUARIUS

(For Christopher Cameron Turco, b. 23 January 1973
—with reference to Burton)

It is anomaly and paradox: Somehow,
   Taurus has sired Aquarius, long,
      lank and fair. He has the father's mouth,
        the same chin, different color,
the original blood born into its own age
      in the first Decan of its Sign.

As"The Soul is an alien to the Body,
   a Nightingale to the air, a Swallow
      in an old house, and Ganymede in
        Heaven, an Elephant at Rome,
a Phoenix in India," just so are Father
      and Son — magnetic opposites.

For blushing "It is good overnight to anoint
   the face with Hare's blood, and in the morning
      to wash it with strawberry and cow-
        slip-water, the juice of distill'd
Lemons, juice of cowcumbers, or to use the seeds
      of Melons, or the kernels of

"Peaches beaten small, or the roots of arum, and
   mixt with wheat bran to bake it in an oven,
      and to crumble it in strawberry-
        water, or to put fresh cheese curds

to a red face." This child is a nugget out of
        middle age, discovered against

odds and medicine; "digg'd out of that broody hill,
    belike, this goodly golden stone is, where
        the ridiculous mouse was brought to
            birth." Perhaps the Bull may drink now,
out of the Water-Bearer's cooling urn. "In the
        belly of a swallow there is

"a stone found called Chelidonius which, if it
    be lapped in fair cloth, and tied to the
        right arm, will cure lunaticks, mad men,
            make them amiable and merry."
Come, Bearer of Water, of Consciousness and God.
        On my arm, bear up your father.

MELANCHOLY LOVE

*Every Lover admires his Mistress, though she be very
deformed of her self,...*—Burton.

"...ill-favored, wrinkled, pimpled, pale,
        red, yellow, tanned, tallow-faced,
have a swollen Juggler's platter-face, or a thin,
        lean, chitty-face, have clouds in her face,
    be crooked, dry, bald, goggle-ey'd, blear-ey'd,

"or with staring eyes, she looks like
        a squis'd cat, hold her head still
awry, heavy, dull, hollow-eyed, black or yel-
        low about the eyes, or squint-eyed, spar-
    row-mouthed, Persean hook-nosed, have a sharp Fox

"nose, a red nose, China flat great
        nose, snub-nose with wide nostrils,
a nose like a promontory, gubber-tushed,
        rotten teeth, black, uneven, brown teeth,
    beetle-browed, a Witch's beard, her breath stink

"all over the room, her nose drop
        winter and summer, with a
Bavarian poke under her chin, lave eared,
        with a long crane's neck, which stands awry
    too, with hanging breasts, dugs like two double

"jugs, or else no dugs, bloody-fain
        fingers, filthy long unpared

nails, scabbed hands or wrists, a tanned skin, a rotten
        carkass, crooked back, she stoops, is lame,
    splay-footed, as slender in the middle

        "as a Cow in the waist, gouty
            legs, her ankles hang over
her shoes, her feet stink, she breeds lice, a mere change-
        ling, a very monster, an auf, im-
    perfect, her whole complexion savours, an

        "harsh voice, incondite gesture, vile
            gait, a vast virago, or
an ugly Tit, a slugg, a fat fustilugs,
        a long lean rawbone, a skeleton,
    a truss," and though she look to another

        "like a merd in a lanthorn, whom
            thou hatest, loathest, and wouldest
have blown thy nose in her bosom, a dowdy,
        a slut, a scold, a nasty, rammy,
    rank, beastly, quean, obscene, bare, beggarly

        "antidote to love," it would seem,
            yet withal to her Lover
is she rather Mother-of-Pearl, not the grey
        clam in brine; the sphere, never the neck;
    she is stinking Venus on the half-shell.

THE MISTRESS OF MELANCHOLY

Let her head be from Prague, paps out of Australia, belly
from France, back from Brabant, hands out of England,
feet from Rhine, buttocks from Switzerland, let her have
the Spanish gait, the Venetian tire, Italian compliment
and endowments.—Burton.

I have waited so long for all the mails to come—
one box Tuesday, another Friday parcel post—
at last I can begin. My screwdriver at *en garde*,
    my mistress first shall get a head: Those perfect
Czechoslovak eyes, Dresden blue, staring up out of

excelsior. Like so, the China throat upon
the Athenian shoulders, soldered without seam.
Now the paps hung, tinkling Bach, upon the Gold Coast chest,
    coasting neatly down to the Riviera.
The thighs from Thailand, smooth as ivory; the Mound of

Venus, straight from Pompeii, sloping invitingly
between Scylla and Charybdis...the Spanish gate.
The kneecaps imported from Hanoi, shins from Vientiane;
    those Aryan toes they floated down the Rhine!
Turn her around to get at the Queensland calves: Clockwork

bums stupendous in their art—one's heart goes running
down to think of the chimes we'll have! Let me get your
back up, honey, this model from Brabant. And now these
    English hands go here, these Wedgewood hands upon
the Remington arms from the good old U.S. of A.—

O Leonardo! Thou shouldst be living at this hour!
My mistress hath tire to strike the Venetians blind!

"A Squis'd Cat"—Burton

Louis Wain (1860-1939), a British artist, was inter-
nationally known for his drawings of cats, characterized
by their almost human expressions and antics. In 1921
Mr. Wain suffered a brain injury in a motor accident,
from which he never fully recovered. From that time—
possibly as a result of his injury, possibly as an artistic
experiment—his cats were transformed from recognizable
household pets to creatures one might see in a nightmare.
                                        —Consuelo Reed.

Melancholy kitty, nice pussy,
sweet pussy. Purr in a corner; lap up your
            milk. Swish your tail, lie on a rug.
Pretty cat in a kitchen. Fur and nice
eyes winking slowly, slowly. Go to

            sleep. Wake up, cat, your eyes are too bright,
a little. What dream was it that made your back
            curve that way around a queer corner? Your
            ears perk like crooked peaks. Hackles
            up, cat; scratch the wall of your saucer.

Squis'd cat, electrical kitten,
symmetrics and fall apart. The paper
room will hold you in place. Triangular tongue
            sharp, not rough: Rakes the eyes, laps blackness
            from a spoon. Where do your whiskers

go? Now, cat, pussy in
a pail, snarl lines and sparks into my ear. My
        eyes wail all your pins and dots, my
    tail does flash, flails behind thy riven head.
   My bowels dissolve,
                 dissolve bad puss;

     see, Fyre Catte,
           drink thy
                nice
                    Night.

THE GOD OF MELANCHOLY: A RELIGIOUS TREATISE

*...he is a rammy, fulsome fellow, a goblin-faced
fellow, he smells, he stinks, he belches onion and garlic,
how like a dizzard, a fool, an ass he looks, how like a
clown he behaves himself!*—Burton.

His feet point inward at
90° angles. The world spins
    between His big toes. He squats
above it all so that the tallest peaks
    just barely miss His ass-

hole. He waits. That's His job,
partly—waiting. And while He waits, things
    get better between His thick
toenails, perhaps. The President goes to
    China; Muhammad goes

to the mountain, conquers
the ultimate crag, never even
    glimpses a hemorrhoid; Dick
puts it to Jane: His wife doesn't suspect
    a thing. But at last it's

time. Deep in His bowels,
Melanchole senses the thin movement
    of gas. There is a small cramp
beneath His duodenum. A tremor
    passes along the San

Andreas Fault. Pressures
build. It is time: There is Agony
        in the Cosmic Expression.
Slowly, our nostrils in the blithe air, we
        begin to understand

        the essence of sulphur,
the quintessence of hopes digested.
        Along our valleys, brown fog
seeps out of the hills. China gags, believes
        it is the President's

        western odor. Boulders
dump Muhammad, and Dick's wife finds out.
        Were we not blinded, we would
understand Joy; were we without noses,
        we would serve no Purpose;

        could we but see beyond
our noses, we would relish delight
        between the toes, under his
cheek—for our Keeper is smiling; nay, He
        is laughing in Relief!

Farewell to Melancholy

*It is most true, the style proclaims the man,
our style dewrays us, & as hunters find their
game by the trace, so is a man descried by
his writings. I have laid myself open (I know
it) in this Treatise, and shall be censured I
doubt not, yet this is some comfort: our cen-
sures are as various as our palates. If I be
taxed, exploded by some, I shall happily be
as much approved & commended by others.*
　　　　　　　　　—Burton.

　If night is staining the window,
　　let the streetlight take care of it,
　　　　washing it into the road
　　　　　　with the neighbors' dreams.
It is March, unseasonably warm

　　in this garret where my clothes hang
　　about my shoulders. Music is
　　　　sneaking out of the books and
　　　　　writhing in the last
cactus. The gerbil has died, but I

　　hear his wheel looming something in
　　and out of shadow. My father,
　　　　whom the mouse has followed, casts
　　　　　a hard stare askance
out of his frame. He is young and

will not forgive me. I can feel
my words crinkle among his ash.
    The new Christbearer under
      me sleeps; the aging
wife; the pubescent girl. I have looked

    into the window and seen what
    the streetlamp can do with plain glass,
      quicksilver, the image of
        a human life, with
night and the past stored in beds, rooms, books,

    in words and silence.

The Compleat Melancholick was designed by Gerald Lange and handset in Monotype Plantin at The Bieler Press. This paperbound edition was lithographically reproduced from proofs of a hand-printed limited edition.

This book was printed on acid-free paper & machine-sewn in signatures to ensure durability & quality of production.